TABLE OF CONTENTS

Preface 1

Ministry of the Spirit 3

Pneumatology 13

Remarkable Manifestations of the Spirit
in South Africa... 19

The Power of the Spirit 31

The Tangibility of the Spirit 37

Christ Liveth in Me... 45

The Baptism of the Holy Ghost 57

Pneumatology
Knowing the Holy Spirit

JOHN G LAKE

GodSounds
"Where Faith is Heard"

Copyright © 2017 GodSounds, Inc.

All rights reserved.

ISBN: 1542500508
ISBN-13: 978-1542500500

For more information on our voiceover services
and to see our online store of Christian audio-books
go to **GodSounds.com**

OTHER BOOKS AVAILABLE BY GODSOUNDS, INC.

Like Precious Faith
by Smith Wigglesworth

Divine Healing: A Gift from God
by John G Lake

Intimacy with Jesus: Verse by Verse from the Song of Songs
by Madame Guyon

A Plain Account of Christian Perfection
by John Wesley

Finney Gold: Words that Helped Birth Revival
by Charles Finney

Closer to God
by Meister Eckhart

The Letters of Ignatius
by Ignatius

The publishing of this book is dedicated to
John G Lake. May his words continue to live
on and bring truth to our Christian lives.

"When He, the Spirit of truth, is come, He will guide you into all truth: for He shall not speak of Himself, but whatsoever He shall hear, *that* shall he speak: and he will shew you things to come." – **Jesus Christ**

Preface

OUTSIDE OF THE BIBLE, I believe this is one of the greatest books on the Holy Spirit available today. It is a compilation of sermons preached by a true Spirit-filled father. John G Lake was a man who studied God as a cosmologist studies the Universe, and he was greatly immersed in the truth of Christ and the reality of God's Spirit in man.

The stories you will read should excite your innermost depths to the possibilities of partnering with the Holy Spirit as Mr. Lake did, for as a truth, God is impartial. What He can do through one, He can do through another, as even Jesus said, "Greater works than these you will do…"

I am hungry and ready for a move of God in our 21st century. The time is coming when His Spirit will be poured out so dramatically, the media will not be able to ignore it. I believe we are on the edge of the greatest revival ever to come to the earth and that God is now looking to see who will be leaders in it. May we not be ignorant of the Holy Spirit, for He is a gift from God and truly reveals Christ through us. Because of unbelief, the Spirit is restrained to move through certain parts of the Church today, which is unacceptable.

May we all come into the fullness of Christ in these latter days and cast off the weights of sin and doubt from our spirits. Let us all declare our trust in God and open our souls to the enormity of His presence. May the Holy Spirit truly fill us so that we all dissolve into the love of the Most High God.

William Crockett
President of GodSounds, Inc.

CHAPTER 1

Ministry of the Spirit

ONE OF THE MOST DIFFICULT THINGS to bring into the spirit of people is that the Spirit of God is a tangible substance, that it is the essence of God's own being.

We are composed of an earthly materiality, that is our bodies are largely a composition of water and earth. This may sound a little crude, but the actual composition of a human being is about sixteen buckets of water and one bucket full of earth. I am glad that there is one bucket full of good mud in us. Water, you know, is a composition of gasses, so you can see how much gas there is in mankind. But we are not all gas.

Now as to the composition of the personality of God, for God has a personality and a being and a substance, God is a Spirit and Spirit is a substance. That is the thing I am trying to emphasize. All heavenly things are of spiritual substance. The body of the angels is of some substance, not the same character of materiality as our own, for ours is an earthly materiality; but the composition of heavenly things is of a heavenly materiality. In other words, heavenly materiality is Spirit. The Word says, "God is a Spirit." He is a Spirit. Therefore, "They that worship Him must worship Him in spirit."

You see, the spirit of man must contact and know the real Spirit of God, know God. We do not know God with our flesh, with our hands, nor with our brains. We know God with our spirit. The knowledge of God that our spirit attains may be conveyed and is conveyed to us through the medium of our mind, through the medium of our brains. The effect of God in our body comes through the medium of the spirit of man through the mind of man into the body of man.

There is a quickening by the Spirit of God so that a man's body, a man's soul or mind, and a man's spirit all alike become blessed, pervaded and filled with the presence of God Himself in us. The Word of God is wonderfully clear along these lines. For instance, the Word of God says that "I will keep him in perfect peace whose mind is stayed on thee" (Isaiah 26:3). Why? "Because he trusteth in thee." That is the rest that a Christian knows whose mind rests in God in real, perfect trust. "I will keep him in perfect peace whose mind is stayed on thee."

The Word of God again says that our flesh shall rejoice. Not our mind, but our very flesh shall rejoice. The presence of God is to be a living presence, not only in the spirit of man, nor in the mind of man alone, but also in the flesh of man, so that God is known in all departments of our life. We know God in our very flesh. We know God in our mind: we know God in our spirit. Bless His precious name.

The medium by which God undertakes to bless the world is through the transmission of Himself. Now the Spirit of God is His own substance, the substance of His being, the very nature and quality of the very presence and being and nature of God. Consequently when we speak of the Spirit of God being transmitted to man and into man, we are not talking about an influence, either spiritual or mental. We are talking about the transmission of the living substance and being of God into your being and into mine. Not a mental effect, but a living substance, the living being and actual life transmitted, imparted, coming from God into your being, into my being. Bless God!

That is the secret of the abundant life of which Jesus spoke. Jesus said, "I am come that ye might have life, and that ye might have it more abundantly," (John 10:10). The reason we have the more abundant life is because that by receiving God into our being all the springs of our being are quickened by His living presence. Consequently, if we are living today and we receive God, we live life in a fuller measure, we live life with a greater energy because we become the recipients of the energy of the living God in addition to our normal energy, through the reception of His being, His nature, His life into ours.

The wonderful measure that the human being is capable of receiving God is demonstrated by some of the incidents in the Word of God. For instance, the most remarkable in the Scriptures is the Transfiguration of Jesus Himself, where with Peter, James, and John the Spirit of God came upon Him so powerfully that it radiated out through His being until His clothes became white and glistening and His face shown as the light.

Now one must be the recipient of the light, glory and power of God before he or she can manifest it. Jesus demonstrated these two facts: the marvelous capacity of the nature of man to receive God into his being, and the marvelous capacity of the nature of man to reveal God. In the glory shining through His clothes, in the glistening of the glory of God that made His face glorious and wonderful, He demonstrated man's capacity to reveal God.

The human being is God's marvelous, wonderful

instrument, the most marvelous and wonderful of all the creation of God in its capacity to receive and reveal God. Paul received so much of God into his being that when men brought handkerchiefs and he took them in his hands, and when the women brought their aprons and handed them to him, the handkerchiefs and aprons became so impregnated with that Living Spirit of God, that living substance of God's being, that when they were carried to one who was sick or possessed of devils, the Word says when they laid the handkerchiefs or aprons on them the Spirit of the living God passed from the handkerchiefs or aprons into the sick man, or into the insane man, and the sick were healed and the devils were cast out.

You see, people have been so in the habit of putting Jesus in a class by Himself that they have failed to recognize that He has made provision for the same living Spirit of God that dwelt in His own life and of which He, Himself, was a living manifestation to inhabit your being and mine just as it inhabited the being of Jesus or Paul.

There is no more marvelous manifestation in the life of Jesus than that manifestation of healing through the Apostle Paul.

You remember the incident of the woman who touched the hem of Jesus' garment knowing how His whole being, His whole nature radiated that wondrous, blessed life of God of which He was Himself the living manifestation. She said within herself, "If I can but touch His garment I shall be healed." So she succeeded, after much effort, to touch the hem of His garment, and as she touched the hem of His garment, there flowed into her body the quickening life stream, and she felt in her body that she was made whole of the plague. And Jesus, being conscious that from Him something had flowed, said to Peter, "Who touched me?" Peter replied, "Why Master, you see the crowd, and do you say, who touched me?" "Oh," He said, "Somebody touched me, for I perceive that virtue has gone out of me." If you will analyze that Greek word you will see it means the life or substance of His being, the quickening, living power of God, the very nature and being of God.

If I transmit to another the virtue of my life, I simply transmit a portion of my life to another, the life power that is in me, blessed be God. The life of God that flows through me is transmitted to another, and so it was with Jesus.

Now then, because of the fact that people brought to Paul handkerchiefs and aprons and they became impregnated with the Spirit of God, and the people were healed when they touched them, it is a demonstration in itself that any material substance can become impregnated with the same living Spirit of God.

In my church in South Africa we published a paper in ten thousand lots. We would have the publishers send them to the tabernacle, and we would lay them out in packages of one or two hundred all around the front of the platform, and at the evening service I would call certain ones of the congregation that I knew to be in contact with the living God to come and kneel around and lay their hands on those packages of papers; and we asked God not alone that the reading matter in the paper might be a blessing to the individual and that the message of Christ come through the words printed on the paper, but we asked God to make the very substance of the paper itself become filled with the Spirit of God, just like the handkerchiefs became filled with the Spirit of God. And if I were in my tabernacle now I could show you thousands of letters in my files from all quarters of the world, from people telling me that when they received our paper, the Spirit came upon them and they were healed, or when they received the paper the joy of God came into their hearts, or they received the paper and were saved unto God.

One woman wrote from South America, who said, "I received your paper. When I received it into my hands my body began to vibrate so I could hardly sit on the chair, and I did not understand it. I laid the paper down, and after awhile I took the paper up again, and as soon as I had it in my hands I shook again. I laid the paper down and took it in my hands a third time, and presently the Spirit of God came upon me so powerfully that I was baptized in the Holy Ghost."

Beloved, don't you see that this message and this quality of the Spirit contains the thing that confuses all the philosophers and all the practice of philosophy in the world? It shows the clearest distinction which characterizes the real religion of Jesus Christ and makes it distinct from all other religions and all other ministries.

The ministry of the Christian is the ministry of the Spirit. He not only ministers words to another but he ministers the Spirit of God. It is the Spirit of God that inhabits the words, that speaks to the spirit of another and reveals Christ in and through him.

In the old days when I was in Africa, I would walk into the native meetings when I did not understand the languages and would listen to the preacher preach for an hour, and I did not understand a word he said. But my soul was blessed by the presence of the Spirit of God.

As Bishop of the church, as I went from place to place holding conferences here and there among white and native people, in many of them, people would speak either in English or Dutch. But I was just as much blessed when a Dutchman spoke and I did not understand him as when an Englishman spoke. Why? Because the thing that blessed my soul was the living Spirit of God. Perhaps I had heard better words than his, perhaps clearer explanation of the Scriptures than he could give, but I was blessed by the presence of God. The thing that the individual was ministering to my soul was the living Spirit of God.

The ministry of the Christian is the ministry of the Spirit. If the Christian cannot minister the Spirit of God, in the true sense he is not a Christian. If he has not the Spirit to minister in the real high sense, he has nothing to minister. Other men have intellectuality, but the Christian is supposed to be the possessor of the Spirit. He possesses something that no other man in the whole world possesses, that is, the Spirit of the living God.

(LETTERS PRESENTED FOR PRAYER)

These letters are to dear people all over the land, and I have this feeling that I would like to revive among us that blessed old practice of believing God for the very substance of the letter, the paper, or handkerchief to become so filled with the Spirit of the Lord God that when it comes into their hands that they would not only feel blessed by the words of the letter, but the blessed Spirit of God would flow into their being out of the substance of the paper itself.

That is Christianity. That is the Gospel of Jesus Christ. That is the thing that goes thousands of miles beyond psychological influence. If you want a clear distinction between psychological religions, as they are called, or mental science, you can see it in a minute. The real Christian ministers the real Spirit of God, the substance of His being. There should never be any misunderstanding along these lines in the minds of any.

A minister of Jesus Christ is as far removed above the realm of psychological influences as heaven is above the earth. Blessed by God. He ministers God Himself into the very spirits and souls and bodies of men. That is the reason that the Christian throws down the bars of his nature and he invites God to come in and take possession of his being. And the incoming of God into our body, into our soul, into our spirit accomplishes marvelous things in the nature of man.

A man came into my healing rooms one day, and said, "I am almost ashamed to call myself a man because I have simply indulged the animal of my nature so that I am more a beast than a man. You say, 'Why don't you quit such a life?' I have not the strength of my being to do so. Unless something takes place that will deliver me from this condition I do not know what I will do."

I tried to show him what the Gospel of Jesus Christ was. I tried to show him that through living in the animal state, thinking animal thoughts, surrounding himself with beastly suggestion, and contacting the spirit of bestiality everywhere that that element had taken such possession that it predominated in the nature. I said, "My son, if the gospel means anything it means there shall be a transference of nature. Instead of this living hell that is present in your being, the living holy God should flow into your life and cast out the devil, dispossess the beast, and reign in your members."

We knelt to pray, and today he came back with tears in his eyes and said, "Mr Lakes, I feel I can shake hands with you now. I am a beast no more, I am a man."

Yesterday a dear woman was present in our afternoon service. She had a tumor that for ten months the physicians believed to be an unborn child. She came with her nurse a few days ago to the healing rooms and told me her symptoms. The thing that fooled the physicians was that there was a movement that they considered similar to life movement, and the result was that during all these months they believed the woman would become a mother until the normal time had long passed. She was the first one to be prayed for after the Thursday afternoon service. Today she returned and said, "Mr Lake, I want you to see me. I have my corsets on. I am perfectly normal. When I went to bed I was not aware that anything had taken place except that the choking had ceased and I felt comfortable. I was not aware of any diminution in my size. But when I awoke this morning I was perfectly normal."

I said, "How did the tumor disappear? Was it in the form of a fluid?" She said, "No, nothing came from my person."

Now I am going to ask you, "Where did a great tumor like that go?" What happened to it? (Voice from the audience: "Dematerialized.")

Yes, the living Spirit of God absolutely dematerialized the tumor, and the process was accomplished in one night while the woman slept. That is one of God's methods of surgical operation, isn't it?

Beloved, the Spirit of God took possession of that dear soul's person. That tumor became filled with the Spirit of God, and the effect of the Spirit of God in that tumor was so mighty, so powerful, that the Spirit of God dissolved it.

That is the secret of the ministry of Jesus Christ. That is the secret of the ministry of Christianity. That is the reason that the real Christian who lives in union with the living God and possesses His Spirit has a ministry that no other man in all the world possesses. That is the reason that the real Christian here has a revelation of Jesus Christ and His almightiness and His power to save that no other human in all the world possesses. Why? He is full and experiences in his own soul the dissolving power of the Spirit of God that takes sin out of his life and makes him a free man in Christ Jesus. Blessed be His name forever.

A few weeks ago a dear woman called me over the telephone and said, "I have a young friend who is a drunkard, and the habit has such power over him that he will go to any excess to obtain. Dry state or no dry state, he has to have it. He is an intelligent fellow. He wants to be free. We have invited him to my home for prayer, and he is here now. I want you to join me in prayer for him." I said, "All right, but first you call one of your neighbors to join you in prayer for this man; then when you are ready, call me on the phone, and Brother Westwood, and Mrs. Peterson, and we will join you in prayer." She called me in a little while, and we united our hearts in prayer for the young man, who was on the other side of the city. About twenty minutes afterward he arose from his knees and with tears in his eyes he took the woman by the hand and said,

"I am a man of sense. I know when something has taken place within me and the appetite has disappeared." That is the ministry of the Spirit, the ministry of God to man. Blessed be His Name.

Isn't it a marvelous, wonderful thing that God has ordained an arrangement whereby man becomes God's own co-partner and co-laborer in the ministry of the Spirit, "the Church which is His body." Just as Jesus Christ was the human body through which the living Spirit was ministered to mankind, so God has arranged that the living Church, not the dead member, but the living Church, alive with the Spirit of the living God, should minister that quickening life to another and thereby become a co-partner, a co-laborer together with God. Blessed be His Name forever.

Men have mystified and philosophized the Gospel of Jesus, but the Gospel is as simple as can be.

Just as God lived and operated through the body of the man, Jesus, so Jesus, the Man on the throne, operated in and through the Christian, also through His Body, the Church, in the world. Just as Jesus was the representative of God the Father, so the Church is the representative of Christ.

And as Jesus yielded Himself unto all righteousness, so the Church should yield herself to do all the will of God.

The secret of Christianity is in being. It is in being a possessor of the nature of Jesus Christ. In other words, it is being Christ in character, Christ in demonstration, Christ in agency of transmission. When a person gives himself to the Lord and becomes a child of God, a Christian, he is a Christ man. All that he does and all that he says from that time forth should be the will and the words and the doing of Jesus, just as absolutely and entirely as He spoke and did the will of the Father.

CHAPTER 2

Pneumatology

THE BLIND RECEIVE THEIR SIGHT, and the lame walk, the lepers are cleansed, and the deaf hear, the dead are raised up, and the poor have the gospel preached to them. - Matthew 11:5

Somebody has lied. Who is it? The preachers of many of the regular churches, theologians, professors in almost every university and college, and the man who has not investigated have all said that the days of miracles are past. We contend that the days of miracles are here now, they always have been here, and always will be here to him who hath faith in God. We contend that God answers prayer today as readily as God ever did; and further, that the same faith that has received an answer once will bring an answer from God again; that the same power of the Spirit of God that moved upon the waters and that performed wonders both in nature and in man, both in the spiritual and the physical, is still available. It is here in Portland. It is at work every day. If you do not believe it, come to our healing rooms and observe for yourself.

THE BLIND RECEIVE THEIR SIGHT

Mr. Adam Streit of St. Johns, Portland, was blind for several years in both eyes. He was ministered to on three different occasions through prayer and the laying on of hands by the ministry of The Church at Portland. He is now perfectly healed and gave public testimony to his healing in The Church at Portland, at 129 4th Street, a few days ago.

THE LAME WALK

A most conspicuous case, Mr. Roy Ferguson, head bookkeeper for the State Industrial Insurance Commission at Salem, the state capital, was stricken with tuberculosis of the bone. The disease affecting the spine, he was encased in a plaster of paris cast and confined to his bed for more than a year. One leg was amputated just below the hip in the hope of checking the progress of the disease, but without avail.

He was abandoned to die by his physicians and brought to Portland specialists who said nothing could be done. He was brought to the healing rooms, was prayed for, and God instantly healed him. He is well. He was saved from his sins and baptized in the Holy Ghost and is now ministering this power of God to others and is one of the representatives of our work in Salem, Oregon.

THE DEAF HEAR

Mrs. Mary Evans of Corvallis, Oregon, was deaf for twenty years. She heard of the healing of Mr. Roy Ferguson through friends and came to Portland to visit the healing rooms. She called Dr. Lake on the phone to come to the Multnomah Hotel parlors where, in the presence of a group of friends and others from the city who were present, she was ministered to and was instantly healed and conversed freely with her friends and Dr. Lake. She reported by long distance phone today that her healing was perfect and she will come to Portland in the near future to give public testimony and praise to God in The Church at Portland.

I, Harley Day, 189 Mill Street, Portland, 18 years and nine months old, being first duly sworn and realizing fully the solemnity of this my oath, do testify: I was born dumb and was thereby unable to speak, also my nasal passages were malformed so that it was impossible for me to breathe through my nose. I under went six surgical operations on my throat, but was not benefited and gave up in despair.

Lately, friends advised me to go to Dr. John G. Lake, divine healer, which I did. Dr. Lake prayed for me at the close of the evening service, laying his hands on my throat. As he prayed, a stream of healing power poured from his hands and diffused itself through my entire person. Instantly something in my throat relaxed and a sense of freedom came upon me. In his prayer Dr. Lake prayed that the dumb demon be cast out. I felt at once that it was done, and in a few minutes I began to speak, and each day I am able to speak with greater clearness.

On another occasion, as prayer was offered and hands laid upon me in faith, my nasal passages opened, and I have been able to breathe through my nose naturally ever since. I have become a sincere Christian and am now a member of Dr. Lake's church and praise my Lord for His saving

grace and healing power.
Signed,
—Harley Day

LEPERS ARE CLEANSED

Mrs. I S of Council Crest, Portland, a beautiful, cultured, high-class woman, became diseased so that a score of physicians and institutions assured her there was no possibility of recovery through medical assistance. The disease progressed until she was a skeleton, her throat became so badly affected from the disease that her power of speech was almost entirely ruined, and her mind became affected. She was brought to the healing rooms, ministered to, and as prayer was offered and hands laid upon her, the power of God came mightily upon her and the disease was destroyed.

There began from that moment a gradual reconstruction of her entire person. She is now in perfect health and soundness of mind, the bloom of wholesome, healthy womanhood in her face, the joy of God in her soul, the peace of God in her heart, and the victory of God in her life. She was baptized in the Holy Spirit and has begun, in turn, to minister the same blessed Spirit to other lives.

THE DEAD ARE RAISED UP

Mrs. W. E. Stoughton, Portland, Oregon, was sick of double pneumonia, hemorrhaging over a pint of blood at one time. We knelt by her bedside while she was in the very throes of death; and even as we prayed, her heart ceased to beat, her respiration stopped, and she lapsed into apparent death. We continued to pray; nine long minutes passed before evidence of returning life was manifest. We continued in faith and prayer, but in less than twenty minutes another lapse came, this time eleven-and-a-half minutes of seeming death, and yet again thirteen minutes, and then came the final struggle when for nineteen minutes no evidence of life was apparent.

We believe that the spirit and body were kept united through the persistent and unwavering faith of those who prayed. At two-thirty in the morning, the glory of God burst from her soul and flooded her with the joy and the presence of God. She was perfectly healed and arose from her bed glorifying God—a well woman.

Her little daughter, Beaulah, was healed of cancer of the mouth after surgeons had said the child's life could only be saved through an operation to remove a portion of the roof of the mouth, which would have destroyed her speech. She was healed through faith in Jesus Christ; not only the cancer disappeared, but she was also healed of leakage of the heart through prayer at The Church at Portland.

THE POOR HAVE THE GOSPEL PREACHED TO THEM

Day by day, we go among the poor and the lame and the halt and the blind, sin-stricken and disease-smitten, ministering God's blessed love and power, fulfilling once more the declaration of Jesus, the mark and stamp of real Christianity, "The poor have the gospel preached to them."

THESE SIGNS SHALL FOLLOW THEM THAT BELIEVE

These signs shall follow them that believe; In my name shall they cast out devils; they shall speak with new tongues; they shall take up serpents; and if they drink any deadly thing, it shall not hurt them; they shall lay hands on the sick, and they shall recover. - (Mark 16:17–18)

CHAPTER 3

Remarkable Manifestations of the Spirit in South Africa

WHILE MINISTERING AT JOHANNESBURG, South Africa, I received an invitation to preach in the City of Pretoria, Transvaal. Consequently, a series of meetings was arranged for. It was my first visit to Pretoria, and the congregation to whom I ministered was a stranger to me. I was entertained at the home of Mr. So-and-so, Hamilton Street. I arrived about three o'clock in the afternoon. About 4:30, a gentleman called and inquired of Mrs. So-and-so if an American stranger was at her house.

She replied, "Yes, Reverend Lake has just arrived this afternoon from Johannesburg." She told him I was an American and had recently come over to Africa. He asked for an interview.

In the course of this interview, he told me that he had

been secretary to Dr. Leyds and acting Secretary of State for the old Transvaal government under Paul Kruger, the last Dutch president of the Transvaal Republic. He told me that when the Boer War closed, because of what he considered faithfulness to the cause he had represented, he refused to sign the agreement recognizing the authority of the British, and in consequence he had been blacklisted as an incorrigible.

This prevented him from obtaining employment. His family had been sent to Europe during the war, and he had no money to bring them back. His property and money had all gone in the cause of the Boers, and he was impoverished. He did not have proper clothes to wear nor food to eat sometimes. He said that, notwithstanding these conditions, his soul was consumed with the problems of state and the desire to alleviate the condition of the Boer people and see the people restored to happiness. In the agony of his soul, he had been in the habit of going into one of the mountains for prayer. After several months of this practice, the Lord revealed to him one day that a great deliverance was coming: that a man would arrive in Pretoria from America on a certain date, and could be found at 75 Hamilton Street, at 4:30 pm.

He said, "This is the date, and I have come in response to the direction of the Spirit, as I received it." He welcomed me as a messenger of the Lord and proceeded to give me the details of the revelation as he had received it. His revelation included political changes that were to transpire, a religious revolution that would grow out of my own work, and many events of national importance, which became historic facts during the next few years.

He further gave prophecy in detail of the European war and Britain's part in it. This was in August 1908.

It was only after I had witnessed event after event come to pass that I became deeply impressed with the real significance of his revelation. He told me that the present meeting I was about to conduct in Pretoria would be marked with extraordinary manifestations of the Spirit, that these manifestations of the Spirit would eventuate in a profound impression of the majesty and power of God upon the minds of the people of South Africa and would create a stimulus of faith in God throughout the world in later years.

Our meeting began at a church on Kerk Street in Pretoria on Thursday night. At the close of the first service, the Spirit of God was deeply manifest upon the people. On Friday afternoon when we assembled, the Spirit of God proceeded to work mightily in the people. Many came to God and confessed their sins. Others who already were Christians sought God with profound earnestness for the real, sanctifying power of God in their lives. Some were baptized in the Holy Spirit, their baptism in the Spirit being marked by speaking in tongues under the power of the Spirit and interpretation of these messages by the Spirit, and also by blessed healings of greatly diseased people.

The meetings ran practically without cessation from then until the following Wednesday at 3 am. Each service marked a decided increase in the presence and power of God.

On Saturday night, the church was packed. All available standing room was occupied with men standing shoulder to shoulder. The majority of those who were standing were men from the Tattersall Racing Club. Most of them were Jews. They included horsemen of all classes—bookies, jockeys, stablemen, racetrack gamblers, etc.

I was preaching on the subject of the power of God and in a strong spirit was endeavoring to demonstrate that Jesus Christ was the same yesterday, today, and forever, that His power was as great as it ever was, and that the only necessary qualification for touching God for anything was faith in Him. The audience was greatly moved.

At this point, I observed a gentleman with two ladies endeavoring to squeeze through the crowds who were standing in the aisles. I asked the crowd to separate, if possible, and permit the ladies to come through and tried to arrange sitting space for them on the steps of the platform. As they approached, I observed that one of the ladies held her arms perfectly stiff and did not move them at all. By instinct, I knew at once that she was a rheumatic cripple. As she approached me, I said, "What is the reason you do not move your arms?"

She replied, "My shoulders are set from rheumatics."

I said, "How long have they been like that?"

She replied, "Ten years." I inquired if she had been treated by physicians. She replied, "I have been discharged from three hospitals as incurable."

I said, "What hospitals?"

She answered, "Kimberly, Johannesburg, and Pretoria."

Then I addressed the gentleman who accompanied her and said, "Do you know this lady?"

He said, "Yes. She is my sister-in-law."

I said, "Do you know her story to be correct?"

He said, "Absolutely." I asked her what she had come for. She replied, "In the hope that the Lord would heal me."

I inquired, "Do you wish me to pray for you for healing?"

She said, "Yes."

Then, addressing the noisy crowd of men in the aisles and around the doors, I said, "You men never saw Jesus heal a person in your life. You do not know anything about this matter. You have never witnessed an exhibition of the power of God and, therefore, should be considerate enough to keep still, confess your ignorance of such matters, and learn. This is what I want. Select two of your company, let them come and examine this woman and see if her arms are stiff, as she states."

I waited for them to make their selection, and they put forward two men. I have forgotten the name of one of the men at this time, but the name of the other was Mr.

Mulluck, a barber, a very intelligent gentleman. His shop was in the market building. I afterward learned he was an American.

They examined the lady critically and found her arms quite immovable, as she had said. Addressing them, I said, "Have you finished your examination, and are you satisfied her condition is as stated?"

They said, "We are."

"Then," I said, "stand back, for I am going to pray for this woman, that the Lord will heal her." Placing my hands on her shoulders, I commanded in the name of Jesus Christ, the Son of God, that this rheumatic devil that bound the woman be cast out and in Christ's name commanded it to go, rebuking it with all the energy of my soul. The power of God lashed through me like a burning fire until the perspiration burst from the woman's face. Then, taking her by the hands, I said, "In the name of Jesus Christ, put your arms up." The right arm went up. Then I said, "In the name of Jesus, put the other arm up, too." She instantly obeyed. Her arms had become free.

As I moved the arm, making the shoulder rotate, I observed that there was a grinding sound in the joint. Addressing the men who had examined her, I said, "You have never heard a dry joint in your life. Come and put your ear to this woman's back while I make her arm move." As they did so, I moved the arm, and the shoulder joints would grind. The oil had not yet returned to the joints.

In the woman's delight, she threw up her hands and praised God and started for the door. The crowd parted for her, and she disappeared, and I did not meet her again for some months.

Another lady arose and came forward, saying, "I wish you would pray for me." I asked her what was the matter, but she did not reply. I bowed my head, saying, "Jesus, show me what is the matter with this woman." Instantly, the Spirit moved my hand down her body from the throat to the stomach, and I prayed for her. She thanked me and sat down.

Later, I learned that her name was Mrs. Ulyate and that she had had a cancer of the stomach. I said to her, "When you came for prayer, why did you not tell me what was the matter with you?"

She said, "I was doubtful whether you were a real man of God or not. I said to myself, 'If he is, then the Lord will show him, and I will not have to tell him what is the matter with me.'" She was perfectly healed. I visited with her and enjoyed the association of the family during the years that followed.

At a later time, her son, a man of twenty, was healed of total deafness in one ear, the result of an eardrum having been absolutely destroyed in an operation. His healing was instantaneous.

THE JABBER FAMILY

On Sunday morning as the service progressed, a gentleman of prominence, who was an employee of the government, came into the meeting, a Mr. Jabber, a man of great statute. As he walked into the church, the Spirit of the Lord fell upon him while he was walking up the aisle, and he fell prostrate on the floor. Several sons were present in the audience, and Mrs. Jabber, his wife, was conducting the choir.

The mother, daughter, and sons gathered from their places in the audience and reverently knelt in a semicircle about him while the audience remained in quiet prayer. The Spirit of the Lord dealt marvelously with him, revealing his sins, and Christ unto salvation.

Presently the Spirit fell upon one of the sons, who fell prostrate by the side of the father, then upon another and another, until the whole family lay prostrate under the power of God. When the Spirit of the Lord had lifted somewhat from them, these sons confessed their disobedience to their parents and to God. And the whole family knelt with their arms around one another, melted by the tenderness of the presence and power of God. Confession and repentance on the part of each to the other made the household of one soul. Words are a poor medium to describe such an event as this. It would have to be seen to be realized. The tenderness and conscious presence of God, the melting power of His mighty Spirit, could only be understood by one who had looked on. No words can tell the story.

Notwithstanding the mighty manifestations of the Spirit, I was anxious that the real working out of the Spirit of God would remove all character of denominational prejudices and those elements in man's nature that keep him from loving and serving God with the broadness in the beauty and grace of holy charity—all that should be utterly removed from the people's hearts.

A PROSTRATE CHOIR

As I was preaching during the afternoon, the Spirit fell on a young lady, Miss Jabber, a cousin of the family aforementioned. She fell from her chair prostrate on the floor, where she remained for a considerable time. The young gentleman who accompanied her and who reverently knelt beside her when she became prostrate was attracted by her desire to speak to him. She said to him, "Send Mr. Lake to me." I ceased preaching and went to her. I asked her what it was she wanted. She said, "Jesus came and talked to me and told me to tell Mr. Lake not to be discouraged, that the power of God will mightily fall upon this meeting tonight."

About four o'clock pm, I left the service and went home to rest. I had been on my feet so long without rest or sleep that it seemed as if I could continue no further. I lay down to nap, saying, "Wake me at 7:30 for the evening service." I fell into a sound sleep, and when it came 7:30, the family reasoned that I was so exhausted, it would be a shame to wake me, and they would endeavor to get through the evening service without my aid.

However, I awoke at 8:00 and hastened to the church. When I arrived, I found that, in view of my absence, the church service was being conducted in their former formal manner instead of the open character of services we had been having. An air of formality pervaded the house. The choir members, about thirty people, were in their places, including the organist, pianist, and director. The choir gallery was arranged with raised steps so that each row of singers sat above the other. The choir chairs were fastened together in sections but were not fastened to the floor.

When I came into the meeting, the pastor who was in charge invited me to preach in his stead. As I preached, my spirit was annoyed by the extreme air of formality that pervaded the meeting, and in my soul I kept praying, "God, do something with this choir. Do something to break up the formality of this service so there may be freedom of the Spirit, so that sinners' hearts may be melted, so that the power of God may descend upon the meeting and the baptism of the Spirit fall."

As this prayer of my soul continued, the Spirit of the Lord suddenly spoke within me, saying, "Go on with your service. I will take care of the choir."

The anointing of the Spirit came upon me, and I spoke with great liberty in the Lord. I was soon so lost in the Spirit that I forgot altogether about the choir, and the formality of the service entirely disappeared. I preached until ten o'clock, when I stepped from the platform and knelt on the floor of the church to pray. An unusual spirit of prayer came upon me, the burden of which was so intense that it caused me to pour out my soul to God in a more than ordinary manner. As I prayed, the Spirit continued to deepen upon me until I was unable to speak in English any longer, and the Spirit caused me to pray in tongues. At such times, the Spirit of the Lord would give me the interpretation of the prayer in English, which would immediately follow the prayer in tongues.

I was lost in prayer but was conscious of a considerable noise. I did not raise my head or open my eyes until the burden of prayer was lifted from my soul. When I looked up, to my amazement, the audience was standing, and at the back of the house, many were standing on their seats, and all were looking toward the choir gallery.

As I turned toward the choir, I saw that the Spirit of the Lord had fallen upon the choir and almost every one of them lay prostrate under the power of the Spirit. When they fell from their seats, they pushed the chairs on the row in front of them forward, so that the front legs of the chairs dropped over the edge of the narrow platform. The whole row would turn upside down on top of those who had already fallen prostrate in front.

The deacons of the church came and gathered the chairs off of the prostrate ones as quickly as possible. The unbelievers in the house were startled and frightened at this manifestation; they arose and rushed out of the door. I instructed the doorkeeper to turn the key in the door and not permit anyone to come in. The awe of God overshadowed the house. I felt it was not time for unbelievers to be present. God wanted to deal with the church.

I went and sat down in the audience. We remained perfectly quiet in prayer for some time. Then, one after another of the prostrate ones began to pray and confess his waywardness and sin to God. There seemed to be but one passion in their souls, to tell out to God the burden of their unbelief, of their sin, their backslidings, and to call on God for forgiveness and restoration and power to overcome. As a soul would thus confess out and pray through into the presence of God, the Spirit of the Lord would lift from him, and he would be permitted to arise. As he did so, he was in a perfectly normal state of mind, excepting that the awe of God's presence and power was mightily realized by each.

Many sat and wept. Others sang for joy. Many were baptized in the Holy Spirit. One young man among the tenor singers lay on the lower platform. Close to him was his sweetheart, a young lady who was a member of the church. Like the others, he was pouring out the confession of his life to God, and to her, telling of his peculiar sins, which were many and vile. Husbands were confessing to wives and wives to husbands, children to their parents, sweethearts to sweethearts, and all to God.

The pianist, Mr. Braun, lay beside the piano stool for possibly an hour, helpless and speechless, as the Spirit of God worked in him. I was moved by the Spirit of God to go to him and pray. As I knelt beside him, my hands involuntarily moved to his chest, and laying my hands on him, I prayed. I did not know why I did so. I just obeyed the guidance of the Spirit. As I prayed, I was conscious of the Spirit of God flowing through me to him.

I returned to my seat, and in about half an hour, he began to pour out his heart to God. When he had finished, he motioned me to come to him. When I reached him, he said, "Send my wife to me." I went to the back of the house, where his wife sat weeping, and brought her to him. She knelt beside him. He put his arms about her and confessed that for three years he had been living in adultery. They wept together for hours. God worked so mightily in them that at three or four in the morning, they returned to their home, praising God together.

The next day at ten o'clock, he called on me to tell me that the Lord had baptized both him and his wife in the Holy Spirit and that when they were baptized, the Spirit of God came upon both and caused them to speak in tongues and praise God in a spirit of prophecy. His soul was aglow.

He said, "When you prayed for me last night, why did you put your hands on my chest?"

I replied, "I do not know. I simply obeyed the impulse of the Spirit."

He asked, "Did you know I was sick and needed healing?"

I said, "No, I did not know it."

"Well," he said, "I want to show you what the Lord has done." And he opened his clothing and showed me a cancer on the chest, saying, "Three years ago when I went into adultery, this cancer appeared on my body within a few days. I have endeavored to hide it from everyone. Even my wife did not know of its existence; no one but my physician knew. But look at it now. See how the power of God has withered it?" It had turned brown as if burned by a fire, and in a few days, it utterly disappeared.

Among other things, the Spirit of the Lord directed Mr. Braun to make restitution to parties with whom he had had dishonest dealings at different times. One that I especially remember was this: he was employed by the government as a civil engineer on a monthly salary. He had been in the practice at intervals of filling out a report saying that he was sick and unable to attend to his duties and would be gone for some days. He was compelled to confess to his superiors that this was not a fact and that he used this time in recreation.

The thoroughness with which God dealt with each and all of these was very remarkable. Lives were cleansed to the very inmost, every sin, both outward and secret. The Spirit of God had taken possession, and natures were changed into the likeness and nature of Jesus Christ.

These meetings were the beginning of a mighty work of God at Pretoria, which continues to this day.

JOHN G LAKE

CHAPTER 4

The Power of the Spirit

THE LIFE OF A CHRISTIAN without the indwelling power of the Spirit in the heart is weariness to the flesh. It is an obedience to commandments and an endeavor to walk according to a pattern that you have no power [of your own] to follow. But bless God, the Christian life that is lived by the impulse of the Spirit of Christ within your soul becomes a joy and a power and a glory. Blessed be God.

The power in the Spirit of Christ only becomes applicable in our life according to the vision and the application of our thought to our own need. The air is filled with electricity. It is in the skies; it is under the water. There is nowhere you can go to escape from it. Consequently, it is usable everywhere, if you take possession of it. So it is with the Spirit of Christ. The mode or means or manner by which the soul of man takes possession of the power of God is through the attitude of the soul and mind of man toward it.

I may live all the days of my life in a quiescent, dreamy state, never becoming conscious of the power of God in my life. On the other hand, I can lend my soul and mind to God in active force until the Spirit of the living God so impregnates my life and flashes from my being that, like the Lord Jesus, the evidences and manifestations of that divine life is given to other men.

One evening in my own tabernacle, a young girl by the name of Hilda Daniels, about sixteen or eighteen, suddenly became overpowered by the Spirit of God. She arose and stood on the platform beside me. I recognized at once that the Lord had given her the message. So I simply stopped preaching and waited while the Spirit of God came upon her. She began to chant in some language I did not know and make gestures like a Mohammedan priest would make when chanting prayers.

Away down in the back of the house, I observed a young East Indian, whom I knew. He became enraptured and commenced to walk gradually up the aisle. No one disturbed him, and he proceeded up the aisle until he got to the front and stood looking into the girl's face with intense amazement.

When her message had ceased, I said to him, "What is it?"

He said, "Oh, she speaks my language."

I said, "What does she say?" And he came up on the platform and stood beside me and gave a gist of her message.

"She tells me that salvation comes from God; that in order to save men, Jesus Christ, who was God, became man; that one man cannot save another; that Mohammed was a man like other men and had no power to save a man from his sins. But Jesus was God, and He had power to impart His Spirit to me and make me like God."

One day, I stood at the railway station in Logansport,

Indiana, waiting for my train. I observed a group of Italian men, apparently laborers, sitting on a bench. They were going out somewhere to work. As I walked up and down the platform, I said, "Oh God, how much I would like to be able to talk to these men about the living Christ and His power to save."

The Spirit said, "You can."

I stepped over to them, and as I approached them, I observed myself commencing to speak in some foreign language. I addressed one of the group, and he instantly answered me in Italian. I asked where he was from, and he replied, "Naples." For fifteen minutes, God let me tell of the truth of Christ and the power of God to that group of Italian laborers, in Italian, a language I had no knowledge of.

Again and again at intervals, God has permitted such things to occur in my life. But, beloved, that is not the real "gift of tongues" yet. It is a little flash, a gleam, but one day there will come from heaven God's blessed shower that will so anoint the souls of men that they will speak in every language man speaks in, by the power of God. The message of the Christ will be given through these anointed hearts to the nations of the world. Said Jesus, "This gospel of the kingdom must first be preached to all nations," etc. (See Matthew 24:14.)

May I refer you once more to history? The Moravian missionaries went to Japan about a hundred years ago. Other missionaries spend long periods trying to acquire the language, but these missionaries, history records, went into a prayer meeting for six weeks, night and day, and came out of that meeting speaking the Japanese languages fluently.

These things only demonstrate to you and me the necessity of keeping the soul open to the ever-growing consciousness of God. Is healing a wonder? No, the marvel is that men have remained blind to the power of God for so long. How is it that you and I, raised in

Christian homes, reading the Word of God, praying to our Father God, failed to comprehend that the power of God through Christ is able to save a man from all his sins and all his sicknesses?

Our souls have caught just a little flash, a little larger revelation of the living God through the blessed Word and through the Holy Spirit, the divine power to make it real. But, my brother, beyond the soul is the great ocean of God. We are just paddling around the edge yet.

When I was ready to leave Pullman last week, my friends gathered around. Many of them said, "Brother, we never heard anything like it. What a marvelous meeting. What numbers of wonderful healings!" But when I got on the train, I sat down and wept. Why? I could remember that back in that town, a dozen people had been prayed for who were not healed at all. They were just as worthy perhaps as the ones who were healed. And, beloved, if Jesus had been down to Pullman instead of Brother Lake, they would all have been healed.

There is a place for you and me, way down at the feet of the Lord Jesus Christ, in humility so deep and true that God can put upon us the real power of God in that holy, heavenly measure that is necessary for the blessing and healing of all men.

Take your umbrellas down. The Spirit is falling. The cry is going up from the souls of men for a new revelation of the power of God through Christ. Bless His name.

Savior? Yes, bless God, Savior from every sin. Do not try to jellyfish your conscience and make yourself believe that you are not sinning, or that there is no sin. No, bless God. There is a power of God so real and true that it will take from your heart every desire for sin and make it so offensive to your soul that your spirit will turn from it. Yes, it will fill you with the Holy Ghost until you rise up a prince and king. Sin gone, sickness gone, the power of God reigning in your life, giving you the glory that was in the face of Jesus, blessed be His name, and putting a song of joy in your heart and the radiant glory of heaven in your life.

Yes, bless God, for this salvation my soul prays, and I pray today that upon this audience the power of God will descend, which will open our consciousness to God and take us into the Holy Ghost and reveal the Christ in us, transforming our nature and making us like Him. Not a little like Him, but in the measure of the stature of the fullness of Christ. (See Ephesians 4:13.) Like Him, like God, like Christ in deed and in truth. God bless you. Amen.

JOHN G LAKE

CHAPTER 5

The Tangibility of the Spirit

It is one of the most difficult things in all the world for people who are not familiar with the ministry of healing to comprehend that the Spirit of God is tangible, actual, a living quantity, just as real as electricity, just as real as any other native force. Yes, and a great deal more so. The life principle that stands behind all manifestations of life everywhere.

Your spirit is the life quality of you, the life principle that gives you action. Not just your mind, but the in-breathed Spirit of God, the breath that God breathed into man. That is eternal. Take this outward man and bury him in the ground, and the worms will eat him. But they will not eat the real man—the one that lives within. So few have any conception of giving that inner man his proper place, or recognize his divine right to rule and govern the whole being.

Now the secret of becoming a Christian is simply that you give God the right to come into your life and indwell your entire being. You have a spirit before God comes in to save you. It is a God-breathed spirit. The eternal, that God breathed into you in the beginning. It took that to make a man of you. That is not salvation. But when Jesus Christ comes into a soul to save a man, His Spirit is born into your nature in saving Grace. He takes possession of your spirit, your soul, and your body, and salvation is the most real thing under heaven. Bless God!

On one occasion I was crossing one of the bridges in Chicago, when a man fell into the river. That was when all the sewage of Chicago went into the river. A man with more presence of mind than I had, grabbed a rope from a dray and succeeded in getting him out, but he was unconscious. A doctor had been called and he put the fellow across a barrel and began to churn him. A gentleman said, "Well thank God, he is saved." But the doctor said, "Not so fast. We have gotten him out of the river; now we must get the river out of him." And he proceeded to get some of that black, inky river out of the man, and get the air into his lungs.

A lot of people in that sense are saved. They have taken hold of God by faith that when they die they will go to heaven, and live with the Lord. But there is a bigger thing than that. The salvation of the Lord Jesus Christ is in "getting the river out of you." Getting the frog pond out of your spirit, so it is pure and sweet like the Spirit of God. Out of your mind so that it is healed, and you have thoughts of God and consciousness of God. All the dirty rotten filths cleansed out of you by the power of God. That is salvation. Jesus never taught any other kind. He taught a salvation for the spirit, for the soul, and for the body, all one glorious manifestation of the redeemed man, Bless God! My heart just rings and my soul just chimes with heaven on that conception of real salvation. That is where the world fell down. That is where the church fell down, when the conception of real salvation deteriorated from that high standard and came down the scale until it was just a squeezing into heaven, and the pungent force of His Redeeming Grace was lost sight of. It has been coming back very gradually.

We who have been following the lessons of the past few weeks in the Old Testament have been getting the foundation truths upon which the whole structure of faith for healing is based—on the experiences of the Patriarchs, on the Covenant that God made with the Children of Israel. "If thou wilt diligently hearken to the voice of the Lord thy God." That is the first principle of healing—obedience to the Will of God.

My, when people get the living in harmony with God and God's Word, they have eliminated nearly one half the causes of diseases already! A man came into my office on Tuesday and said, "O, I am going crazy," I remarked, "Well you look like it." He added, "I feel like going out and drowning myself." I answered, "Sit up like a man and tell me what is the matter with you." He told me, "My wife is trying to leave me." I replied, "Well, the remarkable thing is that she is just trying to leave; it is a wonder that she doesn't just go." "Now," I said, "I will tell you what you need. You need to get down before God and repent of your sin and get right with God. When you do you will be right with your wife and everybody else. Until then you will have hell in your home. It is you that is making it and taking it there." Well, bless God, he did, and he is a saved man and has a saved home, and the family has not gone to wreck.

Yes friends, obedience to the Word of God is the first principle upon which relationship is established.

A lady here had a brother who was dying of dropsy. He came here and began to recover for a week or two, until conviction for sin came, and this absorbed his mind and soul. Then his body began to grow worse. He went clear down to death. Then he threw up his hands and yielded to

God. His soul was satisfied. Then the virtue of the Lord came and healed him.

We are glad God undertakes to save people by any method, but the natural and normal way is to come and confess your sin, and get right with God. You are then on believer's ground, your heart is at rest, your soul is at peace, and you have a consciousness of God's salvation in your spirit. Then faith for healing is natural.

We were ministering to a dear man who was dying of a chronic disease. He kept on dying. After awhile he began to get anxious about his salvation. That anxiety developed until it was absorbing his soul. I said, "There is no use praying for his healing. He will never be healed until his heart comes into rest with God." I told the brother who went out to see him to pray the power of God upon him to save him from sin. When he came back he reported that the sick man's face was aglow. The Lord had come and saved him from his sins and then healed him. "For the law of the spirit of life in Christ Jesus hath made me free from the law of sin and death." In such a Scripture as the above you have one of those wonderfully condensed statements which in a few words reveal the greatest spiritual principles. Another one is, "In the beginning God created the heaven and the earth." Still another is found in 1 Corinthian 8:6, "But to us there is but one God, the Father, of whom are all things, and we in him; and one Lord Jesus Christ, by whom are all things, and we by him." God the original, from Whose life and nature and character and substance Jesus Christ the Creator made all things. So he who prays takes of the Spirit and substance of Christ and by his faith forms or creates his soul's desires, whether for holiness or for health.

Men, by the action of the will, take themselves out of the control of the power of the law of sin and death, and by the action of their will place themselves consciously in union and in touch with the law of the Spirit of Life.

We read of an individual about the Sixteenth Century

who was known as the Flying Monk. The peculiarity was that in certain spiritual states, the man would rise from his chair and float around the room. On one occasion when some royalty was visiting, it is said that he ascended into the air and went out the window. It has been reasoned that this man got himself in contact with some law of levitation, and it lifted him out of his chair and carried him out of the window.

Suppose he could have remained in touch with that law. I wonder where he would have gone?

Back in the Old Testament the prophets went out to look for Elijah. They said, "Peradventure the Spirit of the Lord hath taken him up, and cast him upon some mountain." They were more intelligent about spiritual laws than this generation. But Elisha said, "He is not in the mountains, for when I was down by the river the glory of God came down from heaven, and he stepped into the chariot and has gone on to glory."

We walk through the life with our minds closed, our hearts centered in this old world. How men's hearts and lives are tied to this world. The manager of a theater sent for me, and I prayed for three people in his office. He said, "I have sixteen theaters and every morning I get a report from each institution by telegraph or long distance telephone giving me all the details of the conditions of business. I am just weighted down with it." I said, "Dear Lord, here is a man with his whole nature absorbed in this one thing, the management of a group theaters. He has no vision of God or life or any thing. Here is a man living in that wretched little circle, and all he knows is to keep his theater machine going."

What are you tied to, Brothers or Sisters? A little home along the highway, or on one of those streets? You cannot take it to glory with you. One of these days you are going to die, and there you will leave it and where will you be? Most of us have more consideration for the old house and lot, or a few other trifles than we have for ourselves. Jesus tried to bring that lesson to us by saying, "The life is more than meat, and the body is more than raiment."

The Christian stands out as the revelation of the divine power of Jesus Christ to come into the spirit of man, and change it and make it sweet and lovely like God Himself. To come into the mind of man, and take possession of all its faculties. To come into the nature of man and change it by the power of God until his thoughts are pure, holy, and lovely. To come into his old diseased body until God's action revolutionizes every cell of the blood. I believe that when the Blood of Jesus Christ is applied to a man's nature, spirit, soul and body, that when his sin is forgiven, the effects of that sin should be eliminated from his life. This may not be true in all Christian lives because we have not been educated in our Christian faith to believe with the same force and power for physical cleansing, as we have for the cleansing of our soul. But the Word of God says, "I will cleanse their blood that I have not cleansed: for the Lord dwelleth in Zion." Joel 3:21.

It is a small matter for God to perform that operation. The whole purpose of salvation is to stop the sin and disease process in man. Men live like animals. I do not mean coarsely or vulgarly. They eat, sleep, entertain themselves, labor, but they are not in touch with God at all. Finally man awakens. Like the old colored preacher who was telling of the prodigal son. He said, "He took off his coat and spent that. Then he took of his west and spent that. Then he took off his shirt, and when he took off his shirt, he came to his self." We come to ourselves in various ways.

Benjamin Franklin believed he could bottle electricity. He had a conception that it was real and tangible and could be handled. He believed that the lightning was the same as electricity, so he made a kite and attached a key to the string. With his hand he drew a spark from the key. The result of this experiment revolutionized the world. Men began to study the laws of electricity and to apply them.

Jesus Christ came to reveal the laws of the Spirit and to apply them. In the heart of God there is a dynamic, a power which is great enough to save every man in the world, to heal every sick person in the world—to heal them of anything, of any degree of sin or any degree of sickness, to raise the dead, bless God. This is my conception of what went on in the mind of the Son of God: "To the extent that I can uncover the minds of men, so that they can see this and appropriate it for their benefits, I can save the world." Anyway, that is what He proceeded to work out. So through His life, through His death, through His resurrection from the dead, step by step, He went to the throne of God and presented Himself and received from the Father the Gift of the Holy Ghost. Then He said, "Here it is," and proceeded to bless the world with it. Acts 2. And ever since He has been pouring it out upon the world, upon whosoever would receive it. Bless God!

The Power of God's Spirit will do for you what it has done for any one else in the world. But, beloved, you must come to God with earnestness and sincerity and faith and lay hold of it. Do you suppose that Benjamin Franklin would have discovered electricity if he had not believed there was electricity? You will not get any healing from heaven if you do not believe that there is any for you. You will never get it applied to your body, or your soul or spirit so it will do you any good, until you lay hold of it intelligently and receive it.

That is why we have people testify to what God has done, and try to tell one another of God's action in their lives, until your soul comes into the intelligence of the faith, and you see that the redemption of Jesus Christ was not a mythical matter, but an actual scientific fact. So Christ was not a sentimental dreamer. He had His finger on the keys of the universe. He knew the treasure stored in the soul of the eternal God. He said, "I must bring this to mankind. They must see, feel, experience it. It must take hold of them and change them and revolutionize them." Bless God!

Sitting before me is a man who was healed of rupture. The hernia would leave him in an agony of hell, and he sometimes worked all night to get the organs back in place. He suffered torture for seventeen years. Then one night some friends took him to a cottage meeting. A few saints gathered around and put their hands on him, and the fire of God, that blessing Jesus died for, that Jesus received from the soul of the Father, came down on his soul and body and he got up with his rupture healed. It's a wonderful salvation isn't it?

CHAPTER 6

Christ Liveth in Me

THAT IS THE TEXT, "Christ liveth in me." That is the revelation of this age. That is the discovery of the moment. That is the revolutionizing power of God in the earth. It is the factor that is changing the spirit of religion in the world and the character of Christian faith. It is divine vitalization.

The world is awakening to that marvelous truth, that Christ is not in the heavens only, nor in the atmosphere only, but Christ is in you.

The world lived in darkness for thousands of years. There was just as much electricity in the world then as now. It is not that electricity has just come into being. It was always here. But men have discovered how to utilize it and bless themselves with it.

Christ's indwelling in the human heart is the mystery of mysteries. Paul gave it to the Gentiles as the supreme mystery of all the revelation of God and the finality of all wonder he knew. "Christ in you." "Christ in YOU."

Christ has a purpose in you. Christ's purpose in you is to reveal Himself to you, through you, in you. We repeat over and over that familiar phrase, "The Church which is His body," but if we realized the truth of it and the power of it, this world would be a different place. When the Christian church realizes that they are the tangible, living, pulsating body, flesh and bones and blood and brain of Jesus Christ, and that God is manifesting through each one every minute, and is endeavoring to accomplish His big will for the world through them, not through some other body, then Christian service and responsibility will be understood. Jesus Christ operates through you. He does not operate independently of you, He operates through you. Man and God become united. That is the divine secret of a real Christian life. It is the real union, the real conscious union of man and God. There is no substitute for that relationship. You can manufacture all the ordinances on earth, all the symbols there ever were until you become dazed and you lose yourself in the maze of them, and still you must find God.

There is only one reality. That reality is God. The soul of man must contact God, and unless the spirit of man is truly joined to God there is no such thing as real Christian manifestation. All the processes of preparation, by which a soul is prepared by God for such a manifestation, are only preliminary processes. The final end is that man may reveal God and that God may not only have a place of residence but a right action in the body and spirit of man. Every Spirit-taught man in the world is aware of how gradually his own nature has become subjected to God and His will.

I was visiting with a gentleman who had a grouch on me. He said, "I wrote you a twenty-four page letter, and you have not received it. If you had you would not be here." I laughed. That man has been a Christian for thirty or forty years. Always a devout man, and I have spoken of him frequently to my wife and my friends as one of the most consistent Christian men I ever knew. Yet every once in a while we see how the big human just rises up above the spirit and spoils the beauty and delight and wonder of the life that is revealing God.

God's effort and God's purpose in us is to bring all the conditions of our being into harmony with His will and His mind. God's purpose is not to make an automaton. We see a ventriloquist operating a little wooden dummy, and the wooden dummy's lips move and it looks as though it was talking. It is just moving because another power is moving it.

Now God has a higher purpose than making man an automaton. God's highest is to bring out all the qualities of God in your own soul, to bring out all the individuality that is in your life, not to submerge or destroy, but to change it, to energize it, to enlarge it, until all your individuality and personality and being are of the nature and substance and quality of God.

You notice among the most devout Christians how continuously their thought is limited to that place where they can be exercised or moved by God. But God's best is more than that. Receive the Spirit, then use the Spirit for God's glory.

While I was in Chicago I met a couple of old friends who invited me to dinner. While at dinner the lady, who is a very frank woman, said, "Mr Lake, I have known you so long and have had such close fellowship for so many years, I am able to speak very frankly." I said, "Yes, absolutely." "Well," she said, "there is something I miss about you. For lack of words I am going to put it in Paul's words, 'I bear in my body the marks of the Lord Jesus.' You do not seem to have the marks of Jesus." I said, "That depends whether or not it is the marks of mannerisms. If you are expecting that the personality that God gave me is going to be changed so that I am going to be another fellow and not myself, then you will miss it. If that is the kind of marks you are looking for you will not find them. But if you are expecting to observe a man's flesh and blood and bones and spirit and mind indwelt by God, then you will find them, not a machine, not an automaton, or an imitation, but a clear mind and a pure heart, a son of God in nature and essence.

What is all God's effort with the world but to bring out the real man in the image of Christ, that real man with the knowledge of God, that real man reconstructed until his very substance is the substance of God. And when you stop to reason that to its proper conclusion, that is the only way that Jesus Christ Himself or God the eternal Father will have fellowship with man forever.

When one stops to analyze that fact, we see that God is trying to make us in all our nature and being and habits and thought, in all the structure of our life, just as beautiful and just as real and just as clear-minded and just as strong as Jesus Himself. Than we understand what Christ's redemption means. It is the bringing out of Christ in you, until Christ in you is the One manifest - manifest through your eyes just as God was manifest through the eyes of Jesus, manifest through your touch just as God was manifest through Jesus. It is not a power nor a life separate from yourself but two lives made one, two natures co-joined, two minds operating as one - Christ in you.

In the Chicago conference I sat with an old colored lady one afternoon after the meeting, and she told me of her woes and sicknesses, and they were many. After a time when she had grown somewhat still, I said, "Dear Mother, how long have you been a Christian?" She replied, "Since I was a child." Then I tried to show her that God expected a development of God and His nature and the working and action of God in her in transforming power through the agency of the Holy Spirit, and that there was a process of remaking and remolding that should change her nature and life, and dissolve the rheumatism and Bright's disease and all the other difficulties, just as truly as long ago sin dissolved out of her soul.

After the conversation had gone on to the proper point, I said, "Dear Sister, anybody can see that Christ dwells in your spirit." Her eyes were lovely, delightful. "Let your mind extend just a little bit. Let your thought comprehend that just as Jesus dwells in your spirit and also possesses your soul, in just exactly the same way He is possessing your blood and your kidneys and your old rheumatic bones, and that the very same thing will happen in your bones when you realize that truth as happened in your spirit when you were converted at the altar." (She told me how she had prayed twenty-two days and nights until Christ was revealed in her soul as Savior. She seemed to want to wait twenty-two days and nights for God to manifest Himself in the rheumatic bones, and I was trying to get her away from it.) She said, "Brother, lay your hands on me and pray for me, and I will be healed." I answered, "No, I want you to get well by realizing that right now that same Christ that dwells in your spirit and your soul is in your bones and in your blood and in your brain." Presently the old lady hopped to her feet and said, "My God, He is." She had it. Christ had been imprisoned in her soul and spirit, now He was permitted to manifest in her body.

Brother Tom Hezmalhalch came into a Negro meeting in Los Angeles one day where they were talking about the Baptism of the Holy Ghost. He had picked up a paper and read of these peculiar meetings, and among other things that they spoke in tongues. That was new to him. He said, "If they do, and if it is real, that is an advance in the Spirit of God beyond what is common. I am going to get it." He went, and listened as the old black boy taught. He was trying to develop the thought of conscious cleansing, and he used a beautiful text: "Now ye are clean through the Word which I have spoken unto you." That became very real to Tom, and after a while they were invited to come and kneel at the altar to seek God for the baptism of the Spirit. Tom said unto me, "John, I got up and walked toward that old bench with the realization in my soul of the truth of the Word, and that the real cleansing and Cleanser was in my heart. 'Now are ye clean through the Word which I have spoken unto you.'"

He knelt down and he prayed for a minute or two, his soul arose and his heart believed for the baptism of the Holy Ghost. Then he arose and took one of the front seats. One of the workers said, "Brother, don't stop praying until you are baptized in the Holy Ghost." Mr. Seymour said, "Just leave him alone. He has got it. You wait and see." A few days passed, and one day Tom said the Spirit began to surge through him, and a song of praise in tongues, angelic voice, broke through his lips.

An old preacher came into my office in Africa and said, "Brother Lake, there is something I want to talk to you about. There used to be a very remarkable manifestation in my life. It was the manifestation of tongues and interpretation. But I have not spoken for a year. I wish you would pray for me." I said, "No, go over and lie down, and get still and let God move in your life." I went on writing a letter. Presently I observed that something wanted to speak in me, and I turned my head just a little to see that the old man was speaking in tongues and I was getting the interpretation of it as I wrote the letter.

Don't you know Christians are stumbling every day over that fact. You are doubting and fearing and wondering if Christ is there. Beloved brother and sister, give Him a chance to reveal Himself. He is there. Probably because of your lack of realization your soul is closed and He is not able to reveal Himself. You know God is never able in many to reveal Himself outside of the spirit or soul. The real secret of the ministry of healing is in permitting the grace of God in your heart to flow-out through your hands and your nerves into the outer life. That is the real secret. And one of the greatest works God has to perform is to subject our flesh to God. Many Christians, the deepest Christians who really know God in their spirits and enjoy communion with God, are compelled to wait until there is a process of spiritualization taking place in their bodies before God can reveal Himself through them. Do not imprison Christ in you. Let Him live, let Him manifest, let Him vent through you.

There is one great thing that the world is needing more than anything else, and I am convinced of it every day I live. Mankind has one supreme need, and that is the love of God. The hearts of men are dying for lack of the love of God. I have a sister in Detroit. She came over to Milwaukee to visit us for two or three days at the convention there. As I watched her moving around, I said, "I would like to take her along and just have her love folks." She would not need to preach. You do not need to preach to folks. It is not the words you say that are going to bless them. They need something greater. It is the thing in your soul. They have got to receive it, then their soul will open and there will be a divine response. Give it to them: it is the love of God.

You have seen people who loved someone who would not respond. If there is any hard situation in God's earth, that is it, to really passionately love someone and find no response in them.

I had an English friend and was present at his marriage. Some years later he and his wife came to visit our home. He was the cold type of closed up Englishman, and his wife was the warm type. One day as they started out for a walk, I noticed the passionate yearning in her soul. If he would just say something that was tender, something that would gratify the craving of her nature for affection, but he seemed to go along absolutely unconscious of it. After a while they came back from their walk. I was sitting on the front steps. After the lady had gone into the house, I said, "Hibbs, you are a stiff. How is it possible that you can walk down the street with a woman like your wife and not realize that her heart is craving and crying for you to turn around and do something that shows you love her?" He said, "Do you think that is the difficulty? I will go and do it now." And everything subsided while he proceeded to do it.

What is it men are seeking? What is it their hearts are asking for when they are seeking God? What is their soul crying for? Mankind is separated from God. It may not be mountains of sin between you and God at all. It may be that your nature is closed and unresponsive. My! When the real love touch of God is breathed into your soul, what a transformation takes place. There is probably no more delightful thing on earth than to watch a soul praying into God, when the light of God comes in and the life of God fills the nature and that holy affection that we seek from others finds expression in Him.

That is what the Lord is asking from you, and if you want to gratify the heart of Jesus Christ, that is the only way in all the world to do it. You know the invitation is not "Give Me thine head." The invitation is, "My son, give Me thine heart." That is an affectionate relationship, a real love union in God, a real love union with God. Think of the fineness of God's purpose. He expects that same marvelous spiritual union that is brought to pass between your soul and His own to be extended so that you embrace in that union every other soul around you.

Oh, that is what it means when it talks about being baptized in one spirit, submerged, buried, enveloped and enveloping in the one Spirit of God.

While I was in Milwaukee recently, I went out one morning with Rev. Fockler to make a call on a sick person. We stepped into one of the most distracted homes I have ever been in. A strange condition had developed in one of the daughters, and the household was distressed. They were the saddest group. They were German people. Fockler speaks German. Presently he began to talk to the household. I just sat back and watched. Presently I noticed the faces began to relax and the strain was gone. The girl was apparently insane. She came down the stairs, stood outside the door where she could not be seen except by me. He continued to converse with the family, and as their souls softened and their faith lifted, her eyes commenced to change. She was moved upon by the same Spirit until her nature responded, and in just a little while she stepped into the room. She had tormented that household. Nobody could get near her. She slipped up behind Fockler's chair, stood with her hands on the back of the chair. He understood and disregarded. After a little while she put the other hand on the other shoulder. And in fifteen or twenty minutes we left that home, and there was just as much distinction between the attitude of those dear people when we came in and when we left as between heaven and hell. If hell has a characteristic, it is that of distraction. If heaven has a particular characteristic, it is the presence of God, the calm of God, the power of God, the love of God.

There were days when the church could club men into obedience by preaching hell to them, but that day has long passed. The world has outgrown it. And men are discovering there is only one way and that is the Jesus way. Jesus did not come with a club, but with the great loving heart of the Son of God. He was "moved with compassion".

This morning I lay in bed and wrote a letter, an imaginary letter to a certain individual. I was getting ready so that when I came down I could dictate the sentences that would carve him right. One of the phrases was, "You great big calf, come out of it and be a man." As I lay there I got to thinking, "If Jesus was writing this letter, I wonder what He would write?" But somehow it would not frame. My soul was not in an attitude to produce such a letter. So I came down this morning and called Edna and commenced to dictate, and I was trying to dictate a letter in the Spirit of Jesus. Presently I woke up to the fact that I was putting the crimp into it like a lawyer. After she had written it and laid it down for me to sign, I commenced to read it over. It was not what I wanted to write at all. The first two paragraphs had a touch of the right spirit but that was all. So I laid it aside. Then I went in and prayed a little while. After I had been praying for twenty minutes, the telephone rang. It was that fellow. He wanted me to come down to the Davenport Hotel. We had three of the best hours without being aware of the time.

We boast of our development in God; we speak glowingly of our spiritual experiences, but it is only once in a while that we find ourselves in the real love of God. The greater part of the time we are in ourselves rather than in Him. That evidences just one thing, that Christ has not yet secured that perfect control of our life, that subjection of our nature, that absorption of our individuality, so that He is able to impregnate it and maintain it in Himself. We recede, we draw back, we close up. We imprison our Lord.

The secret of a religious meeting is that it assists men's hearts to open. They become receptive, and the love of God finds vent in their nature for a little while, and they go away saying, "Didn't we have a good time? Wasn't that a splendid meeting?"

I wonder if there is anything that could not be accomplished through that love of God. Paul says there is not. "Love never faileth." That is one infallible state. Try it on your wife, try it on your children, try it on your neighbors.

Ah, sometimes we need to get things over on to the bigger love, the greater heart. It is a good thing to detach your soul. Do not hold people. Do not bind people. Just cut them loose and let God love them. Don't you know we hold people with such a grip when we pray for them that they miss the blessing. Why, you have such a grip on your humanity that it is exercising itself and the spirit is being submerged. Let your soul relax and let the Spirit of God in you find vent. There is no substitute for the love of God. "Christ in you." Oh, you have the capacity to love. All the action of the Spirit of God has its secret there.

I stood on one occasion by a dying woman who was suffering and writhing in awful agony. I had prayed again and again with no results. But this day something just happened inside of me. My soul broke clear down, and I saw that poor soul in a new light. Before I knew it I reached out and gathered her in my arms and hugged her up to my soul, not my bosom. In a minute I knew the real thing had taken place. I laid her back down on the pillow. In five minutes she was well. God was waiting on me until He could get to my soul the sense of that tenderness that was in the Son of God.

That is the reason that His Name is written in imperishable memory. And the Name of Jesus Christ is the most revered Name in earth or sea or sky. And I am eager to get in that category of folks who can manifest the real love of God all the time.

CHAPTER 7

The Baptism of the Holy Ghost

THE BAPTISM OF THE HOLY GHOST is the greatest event in Christian history, greater than the crucifixion, of greater import than the resurrection, greater than the ascension, greater than the glorification. It was the end and finality of crucifixion and resurrection, ascension and glorification.

If Jesus Christ had been crucified and there had been no resurrection, His death would have been without avail, in-so-far as the salvation of mankind is concerned. Or if He had risen from the grave in resurrection, and failed to reach the throne of God, and receive from the Father the Gift of the Holy Ghost, the purpose for which He died, and for which He arose, would have been missed.

It is because there was no failure, it is because Jesus went to the ultimate, to the very throne and heart of God, and secured right out of the heavenly treasury of the

Eternal Soul, the Almighty Spirit, and poured it forth upon the world in divine baptism that we are here tonight.

The Day of Pentecost was the birthday of Christianity. Christianity never existed until the Holy Ghost came from heaven. The ministry of Jesus in the world was His own divine preparation of the world for His ultimate and final ministry. His ultimate and final ministry was to be by the Spirit.

The ministry of Jesus during His earth life was localized by His humanity, localized again in that His message was only given to Israel. But the descent of the Holy Ghost brought to the souls of men a universal ministry of Jesus to every man right from the heart of God. Heavenly contact with the eternal God in power set their nature all aflame for God and with God, exalted their natures into God, and made the recipient God-like. Man became God-like!

There is no subject in all the Word of God that seems to me should be approached with so much holy reverence as the subject of the Baptism of the Holy Ghost. Beloved, my heart bleeds every day of my life when I hear the flippancy with which Christians discuss the Baptism of the Holy Ghost.

When Moses entered into the presence of God at the burning bush, God said, "Put off thy shoes from off thy feet, for the place whereon thou standest is holy ground." How much more so when the individual comes into the presence of God looking for the baptism of the Holy Ghost, and remembers that in order to obtain this gift, Jesus Christ lived in the world, bled on the cross, entered into the darkness of death and hell and the grave, grappled with and strangled that accursed power, came forth again, and finally ascended to heaven in order to secure it for you and me. If there is anything under heaven that ought to command our reverence, our holy reverence, our reverence beyond anything else in the world, it surely is the subject of the baptism of the Holy Ghost.

My! Sometimes my soul is jarred when I hear people flippantly say, "Have you got your baptism?" Supposing that Jesus was on the cross, and we were privileged tonight to look into His face at this hour, I wonder what the feeling of our soul would be? Supposing we were to follow tonight behind the weeping company that bore His dead body and laid it in the tomb, what would our feelings be? Supposing we were to meet Him in the garden, as Mary did, in the glory of His resurrection, or supposing that God in His goodness would let us look into that scene of scenes at the throne of God, when the heavens lifted up their gates, and the Lord of Glory came in. Oh, if we could, beloved, we would have a better comprehension of the baptism of the Holy Ghost.

I love that dear old word "Ghost." The Anglo-Saxon is "Ghest" a spiritual guest, heavenly visitor, spiritual presence, the Angel One. And that Angel One that comes to you and me, comes right out of the heart of the Eternal God, breathed through the soul of Jesus Christ! When He came upon a man originally, as He did upon the hundred and twenty at Jerusalem, no one went around saying: "Brother, have you got your baptism?" They were walking with their shoes off, with uncovered heads and uncovered hearts before the Eternal God!

I believe that the first essential in a real Holy Ghost church and a real Holy Ghost work, is to begin to surround the baptism of the Holy Ghost with that due reverence of God with which an experience so sacred, and that cost such an awful price, should be surrounded.

I sat one day on a kopje in South Africa, in company with a lady, Mrs Dockrell, a beautiful woman of God, baptized in the Holy Ghost. As we sat together on the rocks, meditating and praying, the rest of the company being a little distance away, I observed the Spirit falling upon her powerfully, until she was submerged in the Spirit. Then she began to deliver a message, first in tongues, later giving the interpretation in English, and I listened to the most wonderful lecture on the subject of "reverence" I have ever heard in all my life.

Afterward I said to her: "Tell me what you can about the experience through which you have just passed." She had never been in Europe. But she said, "I was carried by the Spirit somewhere in Europe. I approached a great cathedral." And she went on to describe its architecture. She said: "As I approached the door, I was greeted by an English priest, who led me down the isle to the altar, and I knelt. A white cloud began to settle down, and presently out of the cloud came the face and form of Jesus Christ. The priest was standing in the rostrum and began to speak but I could see by the action of the Spirit that the words he spoke were simply words that were being spoken by the Lord." It has always been one of the sorrows of my life that I did not have a stenographer, who could have taken that wonderful message on reverence for the works of God.

I have been reading one of the most beautiful books I have ever read. It is written by an English lady, Mrs Parker, a missionary to India, and describes the life and teaching and mission of one Sadhu Sundar Singh, an Indian Sadhu. A Sadhu is a holy man, who renounces the world absolutely utterly, never marries, never takes part in any of the affairs of the world, separates himself to religious life, practices meditation on God and the spiritual life. Sundar Singh, when he found the Lord Jesus Christ, conceived the idea of becoming a Christian Sadhu. They walked from place to place. They wore no shoes, they slept on the ground, but their life is utterly abandoned to God.

One of the statements of Mrs Parker, who wrote of Sundar Singh, was to this effect: "As you approach his presence, an awe comes over the soul. It seems as if you are again in the presence of the original Nazarene." Let us approach the Holy of Holies with a similar awe, let us be reverential in the presence of the Glorified One.

The baptism of the Holy Ghost is peculiar to the Lord

Jesus Christ. "I indeed," said John, "baptize you in water unto repentance, but he shall baptize you with the Holy Ghost and with fire; whose fan is in His hand, and He will thoroughly purge His floor, and gather His wheat into the garner; but He will burn up the chaff with unquenchable fire." Jesus Christ, the glorified, must lay His hands on you, and on me, and bestow upon us all His own nature, the outflow of God, the substance of His soul, the quality of His mind, the very being of God Himself. "Know ye not that your body is the temple of the Holy Ghost, which is in you?" A temple of God, a house of God in which God lives!

Sometimes I have tried to get it clear before my soul that God lives in me. I have tried to note the incoming influence and power of that pure, sweet, living Spirit of the Eternal God. I have tried to realize His presence in my spirit, in my soul, in my hands, in my feet, in my person and being - a habitation of God, a habitation of God! God equipping the soul to minister, Himself, God, to the world. God equipping the soul of man that he may live forever in harmony of mind with God. God furnishing to the soul of man the power of His personality, by which man is as made as God. For all the God-like qualities of your heart is due to the fact that God by the Spirit dwells in you. What is it that you look for in another? It is God! You look into the eyes of another to see God. If you fail to see God in the other life, your heart is troubled. You were looking for God.

I am not interested in the form of the figure or the name of an individual. I am interested in seeing God. Is God there? Is God in that man? Is God in that woman? Is it God that speaks? Is it God that moves? Are You seeing God?

The baptism of the Holy Ghost was the incoming of God in personality, in order that the man, through this force, might be moved by God. God lives in him, God speaks through him, God is the impulse of his soul, God has His dwelling place in him.

You may have God. That is the wonder of the baptism of the Holy Ghost. It is not a work of grace, it is God possessing you. Oh, your heart may have been as sinful as the heart of man ever was sinful. But Christ comes to your soul, that spirit of darkness that possessed you goes, and in its stead, a new Spirit comes in, the Spirit of Christ. You have become a new creature, a saved man, a God-filled man.

Sin manifests itself in three ways: in thought, in acts, in nature. Salvation is a complete transformation. God takes possession of man, changes his thoughts, in consequence his acts change, his nature is new. A Christian is not a reformed man. A Christian is a man renewed, remade by the Spirit of God. A Christian is a man indwelt by God - the house of God, the tabernacle of the Most High! Man, indwelt by God, becomes the hands, and the heart, and the feet, and the mind of Jesus Christ. God descends into man, man ascends into God! That is the purpose and power of the baptism in the Holy Ghost. A soul is saved. How does Jesus reach them? Through your hands, through your heart, through your faith. When God baptizes you in the Holy Ghost, He gives you the biggest gift that heaven or earth ever possessed. He gives you Himself! He joins you by the one Spirit to Himself forever.

The requirement is a surrendered heart, a surrendered mind, a surrendered life. From the day that a man becomes a child of God, baptized in the Holy Ghost, it was God's intention through Jesus Christ that that man should be a revelation of Jesus, not of himself any more. From that time on the Christian should be a revelation of Jesus.

If you were looking to know whether a man was baptized in the Holy Ghost or not, what would you look for? You would look for God in him. You would look for a revelation of the personality of God. God in him, God speaking in him, God speaking through him, God using his hands, God using his feet, a mind in harmony with

God, a soul in touch with heaven, a spirit united and unified with and in Jesus Christ!

It is not in my heart to discourage any man, or to make you disbelieve for one minute in the trueness of your own baptism in the Holy Ghost. I believe that God by the Spirit has baptized many in the Holy Ghost. Hundreds and hundreds of people have been baptized in the Holy Ghost during the life of this Church in the last six years. But beloved, we have not comprehended the greatness of God's intent, not that we have not received the Spirit, but our lives have not been sufficiently surrendered to God. We must keep on ascending right to the throne, right into the heart of God, right into the soul of the Glorified.

The common teaching that my heart these days is endeavoring to combat is that God comes to present the individual with a gift of power, and the individual is then supposed to go out and manifest some certain characteristic of power. No! God comes to present you with Himself. "Ye shall receive power after that the Holy Ghost is come upon you."

Jesus went to heaven in order that the very treasury of the heart of the Eternal God might be unlocked for your benefit, and that out of the very soul of the Eternal God, the streams of His life and nature would possess you from the crown of your head to the sole of your feet, and that there would be just as much of the Eternal God in your toe nails and in your brain as each are capable of containing. In other words, from the very soles of your feet to the last hair on the top of your heard, every cell of your being, would be a residence of the Spirit of the living God. Man is made alive by God and with God by the Spirit. And in the truest sense man is the dwelling place of God, the house of God, the tabernacle of the Most High.

Listen! "The words that I speak, I speak not of myself, but the Father that dwelleth in Me." "But the Father that dwelleth in Me." Where did the Eternal Father dwell in Jesus Christ? Why in every part of His being, within and without, in the spirit of Him, in the soul of Him, in the brain of Him, in the body of Him, in the blood of Him, in the bones of Him! Every single, solitary cell of His structure was the dwelling place of God, of God, of God.

When you look for God you do not look on the surface. You look within. When you discern a man to see whether God is in him, you look into the spirit of him, into the soul of him, into the depth of him, and there you see God.

How trifling are the controversies that surround the baptism of the Holy Ghost. Men are debating such trifling issues. For instance, does a man speak in tongues, or does he not? Do not think for a moment that I am discounting the value of tongues. I am not. But beloved, I will tell you what my heart is straining for. Down there at Jerusalem they not only spoke in tongues, but they spoke the languages of the nations. If it was possible for old Peter and old Paul, or for the Jewish nation, then it is possible to every last one, not to speak in tongues alone, as we ordinarily understand that phase, but to speak because God dwells in you and speaks to whomsoever and will in whatever language He desires. And if our present experience in tongues is not satisfying, God bless you, go on into languages, as God meant that you should. Dear ones, I feel the need of that, and I feel it away down in my heart to a depth that hurts. I lived in South Africa for a number of years, where it is commonly said that there are a hundred thousand tribes of native people. Every last one of the hundred thousand speaks a different dialect. These tribes number sometimes as low as ten thousand people and sometimes as high as hundreds of thousands, even millions, of people.

Supposing we were going to undertake to evangelize Africa rapidly. It would be necessary to have a hundred thousand different missionaries and have them all at one time, master one particular language, for there are a hundred thousand of them. No sir! I believe before High

Heaven that when the Spirit of the Eternal God is poured out upon all flesh, that out of the real Christian body will arise a hundred thousand men and women in Africa that will speak in the language of every separate tribe by the power of God.

The unknown tongue of the Spirit was to teach you of God, to be a faith builder in your soul, to take you out into God's big practical endeavor to save the world. And that is the reason, dear ones, that I bring this issue to your soul tonight. In the matter of the baptism of the Holy Ghost we are in a state of the merest infancy of understanding, the merest infancy of divine control, the merest infancy in ability to assimilate our environment, including languages.

When we go to a school we see classes arranged for every grade. I was talking to a young school teacher, who teaches out in the country in a little public school. I said: "How many children have you in your school?" She replied; "fifteen." I asked: "How many grades have you?" She said: "Eight grades." Fifteen scholars divided into eight grades.

The Christian church is God's big school. What student in the eighth grade would think of saying to the child learning its A, B, C's, "You haven't anything. Why don't you have the eighth grade understanding?" Well in due time he will have it. That is the reason the student does not say it. It is because he knows the child will have it. One day that boy will understand just the same as he does. A weak Christianity always wants to drop to the imperfect, and adjust itself to the popular mind. But a real Christianity ever seeks to be made perfect in God, both in character and gifts.

Dear ones, I want to repeat to you tonight a little of my own personal history on the subject of the baptism of the Spirit, for I know it will clarify your soul.

I knelt under a tree when about sixteen years of age, in repentance and prayer, and God came into my soul. I was saved from my sins, and from that day I knew Jesus Christ as a living Savior. There never was a single moment of question about the reality of His incoming into my life as a Savior, for He saved me from my sins. My friends said, "You are baptized in the Holy Ghost."

Sometime later, I think when I was yet under twenty, or there-about, I met a Christian farmer, Nelvin Pratt, who sat down on his plough handles and taught me the subject of sanctification, and God let me enter into that experience. My friends said: "Now surely you are baptized in the Holy Ghost." Later in my life I came under the ministry of George B. Watson, of the Christian and Missionary Alliance, who taught with more clearness and better distinction between the Baptism of the Holy Ghost and sanctification, and I entered into a richer life and a better experience. A beautiful anointing of the Spirit was upon my life.

When the ministry of Healing was opened to me, and I ministered for ten years in the power of God, hundreds and hundreds of people were healed by the power of God during those ten years, and I could feel the conscious flow of the Holy Spirit through my soul and my hands.

But at the end of that ten years I believe I was the hungriest man for God that ever lived. There was such a hunger for God that as I left my offices in Chicago and walked down the street, my soul would break out, and I would cry, "Oh God!" I have had people stop and look at me in wonder. It was the yearning passion of my soul, asking for God in a greater measure than I then knew. But my friends would say: "Mr Lake, you have a beautiful baptism in the Holy Ghost." Yes, it was nice as far as it went, but it was not answering the cry of my heart. I was growing up into a larger understanding of God and my own soul's need. My soul was demanding a greater entrance into God, His love, presence and power.

And then one day an old man strolled into my office, sat down, and in the next half hour he revealed more of the knowledge of God to my soul than I had ever known before. And when he passed out I said: "God bless that old grey head. That man knows more of God than any man I ever met. By the grace of God, if that is what the baptism of the Holy Ghost with tongues does, I am going to possess it." Oh, the wonder of God that was then revealed to my heart!

I went into fasting and prayer and waiting on God for nine months. And one day the glory of God in a new manifestation and a new incoming came to my life. And when the phenomena had passed, and the glory of it remained in my soul, I found that my life began to manifest in the varied range of the gifts of the Spirit. And I spoke in tongues by the power of God, and God flowed through me with a new force. Healings were of a more powerful order. Oh, God lived in me, God manifested in me, God spoke through me. My spirit was deified, and I had a new comprehension of God's will, new discernment of spirit, new revelation of God in me. For nine months everything that I looked at framed itself into poetic verse. I could not look at the trees without it framing itself into a glory poem, of praise. I preached to audiences of thousands night after night and day after day. People came from all over the world to study me. They could not understand. Everything I said was a stream of poetry. It rolled from my soul in that form. My spirit had become a fountain of poetic truth.

Then a new wonder was manifested. My nature became so sensitized that I could lay my hands on any man or woman and tell what organ was diseased, and to what extent, and all about it. I tested it. I went to hospitals where physicians could not diagnose a case, touched a patient and instantly I knew the organ that was diseased, its extent and condition and location. And one day it passed away. A child gets to playing with a toy, and his joy is so wonderful he sometimes forgets to eat.

Oh say, don't you remember when you were first baptized in the Holy Ghost, and you first spoke in tongues, how you bubbled and babbled, it was so wonderful, so amazing? We just wanted to be babies and go on bubbling and exhilarating. And now we are wondering what is the matter. The effervescence seems to have passed away. My! It is a good thing that it did. God is letting your soul down, beloved, into the bed-rock. Right down where your mind is not occupied any more with the manifestation of God. God is trying to get your mind occupied with Himself. God has come into you, now He is drawing you into Himself.

Will you speak in tongues when you are baptized in the Holy Ghost? Yes, you will, but you will do an awful lot more than that, bless God. An awful lot more than that! You will speak with the soul of Jesus Christ. You will feel with the heart of the Son of God. Your heart will beat with a heavenly desire to bless the world, because it is the pulse of Jesus that is throbbing in your soul. And I do not believe there will be a bit of inclination in your heart to turn around another child of God and say: "You are not in my class. I am baptized with the Holy Ghost." That is as foreign to the Spirit of the Son of God as night is from day. Beloved, if you are baptized in the Holy Ghost, there will be a tenderness in your soul so deep that you will never crush the aspiration of another by a single suggestion, but your soul will throb and beat and pulse in love, and your heart will be under that one to lift it up to God and push it out as far into the glory as your faith can send it.

I want to talk with the utmost frankness, and say to you, that tongues have been to me the making of my ministry. It is that peculiar communication with God when God reveals to my soul the truth I utter to you day by day in my ministry. But that time of communication with me is mostly in the night. Many a time I climb out of bed, take my pencil and pad and jot down the beautiful things of God, the wonderful things of God, that He talks cut in my spirit and reveals to my heart.

PNEUMATOLOGY: KNOWING THE HOLY SPIRIT

Many Christians do not understand the significance of tongues, any more than the other man understands the experience of your soul when you are saved from sin. It has taken place in you. It is in your heart, it is in your mind, it is in your being. The man who tries to make you doubt the reality of your touch with God when He saved you out of your sin is foolish. It is established in you. The old Methodists could not explain the experience, but they said: "It is better felt than told." They knew it by internal knowledge. So it is in a real baptism of the Holy Ghost. So it is in prophecy. So it is in healing. So it is in tongues. Do not throw away what you have. Go on to perfection.

The spirit of man has a voice. Do you get that? The spirit of man has a voice. The action of God in your spirit causes your spirit to speak by its voice. In order to make it intelligent to your understanding it has to be repeated in the language that your brain knows. Why? Because there is a language common to the spirit of man, and it is not English, and it is not German, and it is not French, and it is not Italian, or any other of the languages of earth. It is a language of the spirit of man. And oh, what a joy it was when that pent-up, bursting, struggling spirit of yours found it's voice and spake in tongues.

Many a time I have talked to others in the Spirit, by the Spirit, through the medium of tongues, and knew everything that was said to me, but I did not know it with this ear. It was not the sound of their words. It was that undefinable something that made it intelligent. Spirit speaks to spirit, just as mouth speaks to mouth, or as man speaks to man. Your spirit speaks to God. God is Spirit. He answers back. Bless God. And I believe with all my heart that is what Paul had in mind when he talked out the "unknown" tongue. The unknown tongue, that medium of internal revelation of God to you. The common language of the spirit of man, by which God communicates with your spirit.

But if you want to make that medium of internal

revelation of God intelligent to other folks, then it must be translated into the language that they know. That is the reason the apostle says: "Let him that speaketh in tongues pray that he may interpret," that the church may receive edifying. Paul says: "In the church I would rather speak five words with my understanding, that by my voice I might teach others also, than ten thousand words in an unknown tongue." Your revelation from God is given to you in tongues, but you give it forth in the language the people understand.

Beloved, settle it. It is one of the divine mediums and methods of communication between your spirit and God's. And as long as you live, when you talk about tongues, speak with reverence, for it is God. When you talk about healing, speak with reverence, for it is God. When you talk about prophecy, remember it is God.

A German woman came to the healing rooms one day and a brother prayed for her. She had been a school teacher, but had to give up her profession because of her eye sight. She came back some weeks late after having been alone for three weeks. She had never been in a religious service in her life where they speak in tongues, and had not knowledge of the Scriptures on that line. She came back to me with a volume of written material that God had given her. For when she had been prayed for to receive healing, the Spirit of God came upon her and she was baptized in the Holy Ghost. And now God had commenced to reveal Himself to her, teach her of His Word, and of His will, until she filled a volume with written material of her conversations with God. She communed with God in tongues, her spirit speaking to God, but when she came to me I received it in English.

The man that sits along side of you can not understand that. He never talked to God. He does not understand anything about getting up in the middle of the night to write down what God has said to him. Well, he needs something else to convince him that there is a God.

Tongues are for a sign, not to them that believe, but to them that believe not. But prophecy, the out speaking for God, is for all. Therefore, Paul does not want them to crush a man who is speaking in tongues, but to keep their hands off and stand back. Leave him alone with God. Let him travel away out in His love and power, and come back with messages in his soul.

But he must not monopolize the time of hundreds of people in the church with a private communication of God to his soul. But when he has completed his interview with God, he gives forth his knowledge as interpretation or prophecy.

There have been so many controversies over the various gifts of the Spirit as they appeared one after another. Twenty-five or thirty years ago when we began in the ministry of Healing, (this was preached in 1921) we had to fight to keep from being submerged by our opposing brethren in Jesus Christ, who thought you were insane because you suggested that the Lord Jesus Christ could still heal. In the State of Michigan I had to go into the courts to keep some of my friends out of the insane asylum because they believed God could heal without taking pills or some other material stuff. (To popularize healing, some have compromised on the use of medicines, but the real Christian still trusts God alone.)

It was because they did not understand the eternal and invisible nature of God. They had no idea God could be ministered through a man's hands and soul, fill a sick man's body, take possession of and make him whole. The world has had to learn this. It is a science far in advance of so-called material or physical science.

Then that marvelous wave of God came over the country from 1900 to 1906, when hundreds of thousands of people were baptized in the Holy Ghost and spoke in tongues. But listen! Old John Alexander Dowie, riding on the wave of that wonderful manifestation of healing power, wanted to build a church and stamp it with healing only, and his church practically did that, and died. Other churches branded theirs with Holiness only, and died. Others with an anointing of the Holy Ghost, called "baptism," and they died in power also. Later on we wanted to build a great structure and stamp it with tongues. After a while the tongues got dry. Some how the glory and the glow had gone out of them. They became rattly and did not sound right. What was the matter? Nothing wrong with the experience. God had not departed from the life, but was hidden from our view. We were absorbed in phenomena of God, and not in God Himself. Now we must go on. Now beloved, I can see as my spirit discerns the future and reaches out to touch the heart of mankind, and the desire of God, that there is coming from heaven a new manifestation of the Holy Ghost in power, and that new manifestation will be in sweetness, in love, in tenderness, in the power of the Spirit, beyond anything your heart or mine ever saw. The very lightning of God will flash through men's soul. The sons of God will meet the sons of darkness and prevail. Jesus Christ will destroy anti-Christ.

In 1908, I preached at Pretoria, South Africa, when one night God came over my life in such power, in such streams of liquid glory and powers that it flowed consciously off my hands like streams of electricity. I would point my finger at a man, and that stream would strike him. When a man interrupted the meeting, I would point my finger at him and say: "Sit down!" He fell as if struck, and lay for three hours. When he became normal they asked him what happened, and he said, "Something struck me that went straight through me, I thought I was shot."

At two o'clock in the morning I ministered to sixty-five sick who were present. And the streams of God that were pouring through my hands, were so powerful the people would fall as though they were hit. I was troubled because they fell with such violence. And the Spirit said: "You do not need to put your hands on them. Keep your hands a distance away." And when I held my hands a foot from their heads they would crumple and fall in a heap on the floor. They were healed, almost every one.

That was the outward manifestation. That was what the people saw. But beloved, something transpired in my heart that made my soul like the soul of Jesus Christ. Oh, there was such a tenderness, a new-born tenderness of God, that was so wonderful that my heart reached out and cried and wept over men in sin. I could gather them in my arms and love them, and Jesus Christ flowed out of me and delivered them. Drunkards were saved and healed as they stood transfixed looking at me.

During that period men would walk down the isle, and when they came within ten feet of me, I have seen them fall prostrate, one on top of the other. A preacher who had sinned, as he looked at me fell prostrate, was saved, baptized in the Holy Ghost, and stirred the nation with his message of love.

In eighteen months God raised up one hundred white churches in the land. That hundred churches was born in my tabernacle at Johannesburg. The multitude of those who composed that hundred churches were healed or baptized in the Holy Ghost under my own eyes, as I preached or prayed.

I continued in the ministry of healing until I saw hundreds of thousands healed. At last I became tired. I went on healing people day after day, as though I were a machine. And all the time my heart kept asking: "Oh God, let me know yourself better. I want you, my heart wants you, God." Seeing men saved and healed and baptized in the Holy Ghost did not satisfy my growing soul. It was crying for a greater consciousness of God, the withinness of me was yearning for Christ's own life and love. After a while my soul reached the place where I said: "If I can not get God into my soul to satisfy the soul of me, all the rest of this is empty." I had lost interest in it, but if I put my hands on the sick they continued to be healed by the power of God.

I will never forget Spokane, Washington, for during the first six months I was there, God satisfied the cry of my heart, and God came in and my mind opened and my spirit understood afresh, and I was able to tell of God and talk out the heart of me like I never had been able to before. God reached a new depth in my spirit, and revealed new possibilities in God. So beloved, you pray through. Pray through for this church, pray through for this work. Oh! God will come! God will come with more tongues than you have ever heard. God will come with more power than your eyes ever beheld. God will come with waves of heavenly love and sweetness, and blessed be God, your heart will be satisfied in Him.

Will a man speak in tongues when he is baptized in the Holy Ghost? Yes, he will, and he will heal the sick when he is baptized, and he will glorify God out of the spirit of him, with praises more delightful and heavenly than you ever heard. And he will have a majestic bearing. He will look like the Lord Jesus Christ, and he will be like Him. Blessed be God.

The greatest manifestation of the Holy Ghost baptized life ever given to the world was not in the preaching of the apostles, it was not in the wonderful manifestations of God that took place at their hands. It was in the unselfishness manifested by the church. Think of it! Three thousand Holy Ghost baptized Christians in Jerusalem from the Day of Pentecost onward, who loved their neighbor's children as much as their own, who were so anxious for fear their brethren did not have enough to eat, that they sold their estates, and brought the money and laid it at the apostles feet, and said: "Distribute it. Carry the glow and the fire and the wonder of this divine salvation to the whole world." That showed what God had wrought in their hearts. Oh, I wish we could arrive at that place, where this church was baptized in that degree of unselfishness.

That would be a greater manifestation than healing, greater than conversion, greater than baptism in the Holy Ghost, greater than tongues. It would be a manifestation of the love of 1 Corinthians 13, that so many preach about, and do not possess. When a man sells his all for God, and distributes it for the Kingdom's good, it will speak louder of love than the evangelists who harp about love, and oppose tongues and the other gifts of the Spirit.

That was the same Holy Ghost that came upon them and caused them to speak in tongues. No more grabbing for themselves. No more bantering for the biggest possible salary, no more juggling to put themselves and their friends in the most influential positions. All the old characteristics were gone. They were truly saved. Why, their heart was like the heart of Jesus, their soul was like the soul of God, they loved as God loved, they loved the world, they loved sinners so that they gave their all to save them.

Do you want Him? You can have Him. Oh! He will come and fill your soul. Oh, the Holy Ghost will take possession of your life. He will reveal the wonder of heaven and the glory of God, and the richness and purity of His holiness, and make you sweet and God-like forever.

Prayer in Tongues and Interpretation:

Thou art not far away, Oh God, Our souls tonight are enveloped in the Eternal God. We feel thee round about us. We feel thy precious loving arm, and the beating of thy heart, and the pulsing of thy heavenly soul, and we are asking thee, my God, that the truth of the Eternal shall be breathed into us forever until all our nature is submerged in God, buried up in God, in filled with God, revealing God.

Printed in Great Britain
by Amazon